This guide belongs to

_____

Instagram IS for Bosses.

I mean, there is so much opportunity there, I get excited each time I

think about another way to monetize a stream of income using the

platform.

For me, it began way back on Myspace.

My very first account was for my first company, PoshLifeBling, which

I started in my living room, and took to the red carpet! And I started

that company without a single penny. Pure creativity and desire.

Desire to be more, do more, and have more.

Since then, I have worked inside of the "celebrity world". Building

relationships and even sometimes partnering up with some of the

biggest brands of the last decade. I've seen a lot. I've paid such close

attention to how Influence works.

And I've taken that influential blueprint and followed it to the letter, to create a thriving brand. Two thriving brands, in fact. I'm going to share what I've figured out with you.

Let's take a look at one of my clients + favorite families to watch - because I'm in awe of what they have created since I met Khloe back just about 4 months before the show aired...

I wrote this book because I want you to see the potential. I want you to see possibility, and know that Instagram provides an opportunity for new business hopefuls to create their dream life.

Much like YouTube and MySpace did for people in the early 2k's. And perhaps on an even greater scale. Instagram presents opportunity like never before.

As you go through this guide, think about the possibility.

Open your mind and heart to possibility; to all the amazing opportunity that you can create – if you're willing to be a part of that small percentage...who's willing and committed to making it happen for yourself. It's the new land of opportunity. And everything IS possible.

XO, Tori

Table of Contents

Instagram for Business:

Introduction

I've dissected The Kardashian Sales Funnel.

I already know…

You have to be thinking the same thing I was when I first dissected this, so go with me here.

As a Business Coach + Mentor who specifically works with ecommerce startups using Instagram as a marketing platform, this is one of the coolest things I've ever broken down.

Everyday people are using Instagram for far more than just a place to post the photos of what's happening in their daily lives.

Many, in fact, are taking it and creating Lifestyle Brands (the Kardashians — *just pick one*).

Beauty Influencers (*@HudaBeauty*) have become household names, and everyday people have used it to become powerhouse clothing brands (*@FashionNova*) all from simply creating a place where people want to come and get involved in what they have to offer.

Legit, *daily*.

They WANT to interact.

They WANT to check in daily to see what's been posted.

They NEED to be a part of what those brands do and have whatever they put out for sale. There's an intentional, tactical reason behind all of that.

These brands have essentially found strategies that work specifically for each of them that make people come back every single day to check for them.

It's not accidental.

It's **Strategic and Intentional.**

Recently, I heard Kim Kardashian on an episode of their show, *"Keeping Up with The Kardashians"*, say that Kanye actually gets upset about the order of things she posts on her timeline.

 My first thought was, *"how ridiculous, Kanye"* (*judging much, lol*).

But then, just as quickly, the business person in me quickly switched to -*"F*cking Ye' is creating a strategic timeline **even** for Kim Kardashian!"*

She's an **Iconic** celebrity, and they get that there's still **strategy** necessary — **even for Kim** — because they've had their entire audience in an ongoing sales funnel for the last **decade!**

Let that sink all the way in.

This is very exciting for business owners or startups.

Think about Kim's story.

She was once Paris Hilton's sidekick; ***no story, no interest, no value to speak of (relative to consumer interest, obviously).***

Next...

She made the infamous tape ➡ **Lead Magnet**

She began showing up on the scene everywhere and got her own television show ➡**Email Sequence**

Then came the store, DASH ➡**Product Offer**

She introduced Kimoji's + her APP and developed her own line of Makeup ➡ **Upsell**

Passive income is what we can continue to expect, from every new generation watching those reruns…and it'll show up in multiple revenue streams ➡ *That is*:

The APP, makeup, stores, etc.,which will continue to sell as long as they have episodes on repeat on E!

And of course, there are her **additional revenue streams** ➡ Appearances, Events, Collaborations + Brand Partnerships

And all of this centers around a television show; but *mainly* around their **social media**.

Because social media is where fans go for daily interaction and updates.

So the **Instagram feed**, more than Snapchat even, because that goes away after 24 hours, becomes the **brand presence** for Kim; and each one of the Kardashian's in fact.

Not the tv show.

Not the website.

Not the press.

And Kanye, in all his artistic specificity…*gets it*.
Knowing this essentially changes the game for the everyday startup.

Because the truth is, **you don't have to be a Kardashian** to have business success using Instagram as your "home page" and the base of operations.

That is; using the platform as a place to create a powerful presence and draw your dream customer to you daily.

You simply need to understand exactly what's happening behind the scenes.

You have to understand that social media, Instagram specifically, creates a very unique opportunity for businesses.

More and more, I see major celebrities on these platforms, creating new streams of income. Seriously, J.Lo just started her own personal YouTube channel…because even they recognize that the HudaBeauty's + Fashion Nova's have essentially created multi-million dollar brands…all *without* the "celebrity" *using social media*.

So imagine what **their existing celebrity** can do for them…without any middle parties involved.

The Influential brands I mentioned before have used the platforms to show their brand identity, connect to their target audience, deliver consistent value through their content, connect + interact, engage, show lifestyle, and *monetize the sh*t out of social media platforms*!

What I love most about Instagram is the OPPORTUNITY it gives everyday people to create a unique space in their industry.

It levels the playing field between big brands + the everyday person.

Between celebrities + influencers.

Across gender, race, religion.

Instagram is the new "Land of Opportunity"!

I've covered the Kardashian Sales Funnel in one of my trainings for many reasons...let's recap:

The Instagram feed is the base of Kim K's operations:

For businesses like yours + mine that creates the opportunity on Insta for you to stake your "land".

Insert image of Tom Cruise + Nicole Kidman running for their piece of land in *Far and Away* (1992)!

My obsession with the KSF lies in understanding that it doesn't matter who you are or what service you provide (*assuming it's legal for Instagram*), you can create your unique space where you will:

1. Attract your dream customer.

2. Deliver value to them that only your business can.

3. Build a relationship with them.

4. Nurture that relationship (while building other ones).

5. Present them with the solutions that your business alone can deliver them.

No two businesses will run exactly the same.

They will use the same systems, but they will each have their way of implementing that system.

If you're looking to create the exact strategy as others, it simply doesn't work. Same if they're wanting to recreate yours.

And yet, if you take the systems and apply them to your brand strategy, everything begins to align.

Quotes are big on Instagram

But they don't work for every brand the same way.

Branded graphics give businesses a way to connect with THEIR audiences. So you're taking your brand values + message + tone = IDENTITY.

This is how a consumer or client will connect with you vs. others in your industry.

Your Instagram feed becomes the entry point for your dream customer. It's the place where you get to make an Impact + Impression = Authenticity!

Don't waste time being someone you are not!

Audiences want to connect with brands that really represent their own thoughts + feelings; KLT (Know, like, trust).

The success of your business lies in finding the niche market you'll operate in.

It's how you'll be the "authority"; because this is something that no other company can replicate.

Notes + Thoughts:

Instagram for Business:

I. *The Struggle*

I. The Struggle

They say the struggle is real for entrepreneurs, especially just starting out on the Instagram platform. That struggle would include several elements of what entrepreneurs are facing now when building their businesses.

Let's face it, there is a lot of competition online, especially if you are just beginning your business.

If you have never run an ecommerce business, if you have never sold a product using a social media platform, you're especially facing the learning curve. There is a struggle ahead when you think about competition This isn't to say that success for you is impossible.

But there is a common misconception about what's needed to reach success.

Many are unrealistic about what there is to face with building a product offer; especially if you are in a market that is saturated or tougher to get into.

That is not to say that you should lose hope, that you should give up, or that you should not pursue the thing that you are passionate about.

Because the reality is, your success will be directly linked to the work that you are willing to put in.

The struggle also becomes real for many entrepreneurs starting a business because of the doubt that can creep in in the form of Imposter Syndrome and impede any hope that you have of pursuing your dreams.

Mainly because your overall fear of failure becomes bigger than your desire to have the life you're wanting and know you were meant to lead.

And if you allow it, that thought will permeate every single corner of your mind. You create scenarios and perceived happenings that really aren't even there.

Why does this matter?

So often, people have it in their minds that someone is hating on them, or that someone dislikes them or every single thing that someone (perhaps a competitor) posts on social media directly relates to them.

When in reality, the person is not thinking about you, haven't thought about you, and literally it has *nothing* to do with you.

Of course, there are the actual haters. Those who are paying attention to what you are doing, how you're executing, the systems you use; those "fans" who have a thought about every single move that you make.

They judge every single move you make and have a comment to add every single time you make a move on social media.

They use your entire business model as their playbook, to decide what content they will post and what products they will sell, and essentially becoming the *anti— you* with every move that they make.

If you have an opinion, they say the exact opposite just to drum up drama or competition. *It's out there!*

And then there is family… *gotta love your families.*
They will have an opinion on just about everything, whether you asked for that opinion or never even considered it.

They will want to know what you are working on, they may feign interest to pacify you.

They may be completely disinterested. They may have a and opinion about every single moment that you spend on social media.

They may just not get it.

Getting information becomes a struggle…

Because of course, everyone's an expert!

Everyone has all the answers *(whether they've done it or not)* and everyone, in their quest to be the next big thing, has something to tell you about how to do it.

And finally....

There is the struggle of time.

Time is one of the biggest and worst enemies of every entrepreneur for many reasons.

But mainly, because everyone wishes for more of it and the hard truth is that every single day we are all using it up.

So I wrote this book because I don't want you to focus on the struggle.

Because the struggle *does not* have to be real.

Sure, there will be competition.

But that is precisely why there are *niche markets*. And niche markets sell products.

When you can find your unique place in any industry, there is no such thing as competition because no one can *do you* the way that ***you do***.

No one knows your product the way that you do. No one has your brain. No one has ***your experiences.***
And no one can bring a product to market the way that you can.

What I've learned is there really isn't anything new under the sun when it comes to business. People have been selling for centuries.

And when you think about social interaction, think back to the beginning of television, to the beginning of Hollywood.

As far back as you can place this industry of social interaction through any means.

And while the mediums and platforms may change, the reality is; the systems are very much the same.

The differences lie in the availability of information and the amount of information that is available about a specific subject.

Fortunately for you, information is available in abundance in this digital age.

So weeding through to find the right source for your needs really is your main issue.

Even that can be resolved through developing social proof and finding social proof for the sources that you get your information from.

What should excite you and make you extremely hopeful is the fact that the scales between celebrity and influence have balanced for the everyday person looking to create influence to grow their income using social media; Instagram specifically for their business.

Opportunities now exist in such abundance to reach hundreds and thousands and millions of people every single day through the use of social media.

So essentially...there is no such thing as a crowded market. ***Only untapped niches.*** There's no such thing as not being able to sell a product that interests and excites you, and getting into a business that you are super excited about.

It does not exist because there are literally billions of people in the world who have so many differences.

And at the very same time, those people also have things in common with you and your ideal customer that can bring them to you and essentially lead you to unparalleled income earning potential.

So be excited and encouraged, because *the struggle is not real*.

In fact…*the struggle does not exist*.

The key to creating your niche is finding what you are passionate about.

Think about the fact that you'll be spending lots of time working very long hours up front before any sales come in, before you really see traction - in the building phase!

So you'll want to get very clear on your niche market and exactly what the product/service is that you'll be providing. What does that specific person look like? What will you help them transform to?

You may have an idea of who you serve or the product you offer...but since this is such an important part of your business, you'll be getting very crystal clear + specific here.

Who are your target clients? If you say "everyone" you are making a very big mistake. Identifying pillars of your brand will help you with daily content + conversations with your audience.

This is the content that you will use in your feed, stories, IGTV, ebooks, blogs, and emails. This is the content that you will use when making your sales offers.

Brand Pillars are essential to bringing customers into your business. It's the way that people identify how you're the person that they want to learn from or shop with.

These will relate back to what you sell. For example, mine are: Brand, Content, Monetize, Growth, Influence.

So I can talk around any of those subjects, because I know so much about each one. And they relate to the products I sell. Let's identify yours.

The first thing you'll do is identify your passion and make them evident through your brand pillars.

This becomes the foundation for your content creation + daily interaction with your community + followers. It's essential to your audience growth + reaching the right, targeted people each day.

Let's talk about your Unique Selling Proposition: Before you can begin to sell your product or service to anyone else, you have to sell yourself on it.

This is especially important when your product or service is similar to those around you.

Very few businesses are one-of-a-kind. Unless you can pinpoint what makes your business unique in a world of competitors, you cannot target your sales efforts successfully.

Pinpointing your USP requires some hard soul-searching and creativity.

What I love the most...

It's the thing you have that no one else does, that no one can replicate.

Develop your USP from your passions and personal experiences.

You know what you love to do + are passionate about. It's the thing you wake up wanting to do. It's the excitement you feel when performing a certain task.

Or the pride you feel and accomplishment that resonates when reaching a desired result from the effort you put in.

Identify the unique gifts that you have to position yourself in your industry as the person your dream customer wants + needs to get it from.

In fact, there can be millions of other people who offer **what you do...but they ONLY want it from you!**

Be specific about your experiences.

Think about the topics/ subjects that you can speak on ongoing.

Think about how that experience brought you to be the person you are - and to offer the product that you're selling.

Take this and see how it can apply to a unique, niche market...

A HERO that can be the main focus of your product/ dream customer.

Notes + Thoughts:

_____

_____

_____

_____

_____

_____

_____

Instagram for Business:

II. *Dream Customers*

II. Dream Customer

There are so many ways to reach your ideal customer. Your dream customer is not someone you have to chase around on social media.

You should not have to stress over finding the right person to sell your product to. You should not spend hundreds and thousands of dollars in ads at start up to reach those audiences to begin seeing an income.

Your ideal customer finds you through your USP; that is, unique selling proposition. You can think I am funny, upbeat, friendly, outgoing and bubbly. And yet, that would not be the thing that would make you purchase this book.

Because while that is great, that doesn't help you with the individual solution that you are seeking.

What you would be looking for is a combination of those personality traits mixed with my expertise and my history.

And that is something that is *exclusive to me*.

So while there may be many other coaches, business experts, brand builders… they are not me.

You sought out a specific combination of factors and personality traits, mixed with expertise I have acquired over this 17 years in business.

That combination is something that exclusively I have that other people can't duplicate.

Perhaps you're wanting to build a luxury brand specifically.

Perhaps you want to learn how to work with celebrities and in doing so, you have come to me to find out how I've done that because there is a lot of money to be made for being associated with celebrities and big Brands.

So yes, lots of coaches. Lots of strategists. Lots of brand builders.

But they differ than the combination that I have.

That's why you chose me. U.S.P.

This is the same for your business, too. Niche-based is the key to your business success.

If you try to talk to *everyone*, you are talking to **no one**.

In my Kardashian Sales Funnel, I talked about the lead magnet for Kim, which essentially is the infamous video.

The video brought interest to her for her to then create the influence that she needed to then go on to begin her *"email sequence"*, which is the television show, *"Keeping Up With The Kardashians"*.

There's a very specific and uniquely defined audience that's going to relate to her because of the fact that her fame was skyrocketed from her video.

So instantly, that lead magnet begins to break down the audience and identifies her ideal, dream customer.

That is what the lead magnet does for any business, any niche, any market that you can think of. There should be a draw and something of interest that the audience gets to sample.

That can be something salacious, it can be something informative, something emotionally charged, or something that helps your audience use your product *better*.

Each business needs a value product that allows the customer to connect to your brand specifically.

It can be something as simple as a sample, or taste of that item. When's the last time that you were in a Sam's Club, BJ's, or even in a grocery store where they have stations set up for you to sample the goods.

Why? So that you can see the value in the item. This is their value to you as the consumer. They aren't waiting for you to purchase the product.

The company has such faith and confidence in their product, that they are more than happy to have you sample it at no cost, so that you can see that value.

The sampling is the lead magnet.

Your lead magnet will draw people into your email sequence.

For the last decade plus, we have been trapped inside of a Kardashian Sales Funnel.

And I'm going to break this down into a simple formula you can use for your business model to sell more products with a simple selling formula.

Let's look at hair brands. I use the term brand loosely here.

They show up on Instagram daily. In fact, I see far more in my feed than I ever want to, because I do have many of them inside of the PGC Community.

Many people go into this business because they think it's easy to get the products, easy to post photos of themselves or even other women wearing the hair extensions, so that translates to easy money.

Once they get into the business and have a few samples purchased, and a cute page with pretty faces strewn about, they realize it isn't a simple market to contend in. Is it a saturated market?

Perhaps. But the amount of competition isn't the issue. The METHOD people use to sell hair is saturated!

Same photos of hair extensions all over their page.

Same customer they are targeting: Glam girls/ beauty girls/ businesswomen.

Instead of…

Identifying a unique market that no one else has considered!

- Drag Queens

- Cancer Patients (Cause Driven)

- Positioning as the most affordable for the "everyday girl"

- Making it affordable with a membership that people can "invest in" each month

What is your *unique* experience with your market?

Take this expertise + experience, combine it with your niche market = SELLING PROPOSITION

How you will get customers to buy from you.

Identify the aspects of your product or service that competitors cannot imitate. This is where your magic happens.

How do you take the "Hero", or person they relate to in your sales copy, from point a to z? You do this in the Hero's journey.

Notes + Thoughts

Instagram for Business:

III. *The Hero*

III. The Hero

Let's talk about the hero; the person who will need, want, and desire a solution from you.

So the hero of any story or any business model is essentially the person who wants to fulfill a goal or dream. Alternatively, they're lacking something that only you can supply.

The hero is the focus of the story.

You can always be the hero of your story if you are the influencer, or the person who has been transformed by the circumstances that brought you to offer a specific product or service.

Or, your hero can be a specific client that you serve (the hero representing that person in multitudes of people) who again, you offer a solution for.

The Hero has a specific goal they want to achieve.

That breaks down in many ways for different businesses.

Example I:

You are an It Works Reseller. You offer all of the products, but none seem to be selling.

What can you possibly be doing wrong?

1. Posting the same photos of the "dream customer" using the belly wraps.

2. Using/ posting the same images of the products from their website that are supplied in stock photos.

3. Using the same captions + "sales copy" that doesn't sell this type of product.

__What can you do to sell this product smarter using__

__Instagram?__

1. Never post the belly photos. Like ever. Instead, imagine the girl that you're targeting who's the Hero of your story. What does she do? Who does she want to be? When she's transformed, what are the types of activities will she be involved in? What's the LIFESTYLE she wants to live? That is reflected in your Instagram feed. You'd show how she's using this in her day to day life.

2. That can break down to photos and videos at the gym. Or create a viral campaign with your clients

+ customers that they can join in your branded hashtags. Let them create UGC, or User Generated Content, that you then repost into your feed. Or your IG stories. You can, in contrast, have users share your feed/ branded content with their audiences displaying lifestyle over products in the images.

3. Product images are interesting. They usually fall flat and miss the mark when it comes to showing the customer what they want to see that inspires a feeling within, to move them into a purchase. This feeling can easily be achieved through the use of the right imagery. Stock photos rarely, if ever, resonate with your audience because they are generic and intended to serve masses, not the individual. Think of them as placeholders. Not as

targeted graphics that your customer can identify themselves in your business.

4. The sales copy, or written captions, serve the same purpose as the graphics. They're intended to specifically address the dream customer. Not everyone, in a generic tone. As you write captions, think about what the goal is for that specific caption is. What is the intended conversion?

- Sales? Less likes - more focused on getting the right customer to comment, inquire, purchase

- Likes? Vanity metrics.

- Reach + virality: For popularity + advertising opportunities for the page.

- Comments/ Traffic? : For running contests or impressing a brand, use for *sfs's* (shout for shouts: posting content on your feed for other companies, and they do the same for you for a period of time) + giveaways or if you're running campaigns for other brands. Or if you're submitting a request to be a Brand Ambassador or Influencer. Show what your engagement can look like.

- Lead Generation? Here, you're more focused on viral content that will bring in tons of likes + followers for your audience. So you always have to consider (with every post in fact) exactly what the best content is for your audience. So when you make a post, you can bring in more of the right people who resonate with the message on each one that you put on your feed. And, there's no wasted time or effort.

The takeaway here in this lesson, is that no matter who your Hero is - for that post, that product, or your brand; they are clear + present in representation for every single post.

How can you demonstrate to your customers that you have this experience?

Social proof…

- Reviews

- Certificates

- Education

- Experience

You should have your passion identified and evident through your brand pillars. This becomes the foundation for your content creation + daily interaction with your community + followers. It's essential to your audience growth + reaching the right, targeted people each day.

Notes + Thoughts

_____

_____

_____

_____

_____

Instagram for Business:

iv. *Brand Identity*

IV. YOUR PASSIONS IN CHECK, NOW: Brand Identity.

Brand Identity is the way your business comes to life visually. It's logo, graphics, branded content (like your own individual quotes made with your branding), that identify and distinguish the brand in consumers' minds.

Building a positive brand image can bring in consistent sales and make product roll-outs more successful.

Brand image is the actual result of these efforts, successful or unsuccessful.

What does that mean, exactly?

If it's a business page, whatever you post on your feed is how people see your business.

It's all about developing your visual graphics.

Write a list of some of the types of visuals you can use to develop a feed that's more appealing to your audience.

Then, go find at least 30 images, enough for a single post per day (although you should definitely be posting more than this).

And create your own graphics that add value to your visitors based on what YOU do!

Then attach long form, value posts to those graphics.

That becomes your sales copy!

When you brand yourself properly…

And work in YOUR zone of genius…You attract your Dream customer.

That is the whole purpose of...

1. Creating your niche market.

2. Developing your USP.

3. Branding for YOUR ideal customer (the hero).

This is the person that your ideal customer, your dream customer, will relate to and see themselves as.

They will be the one that you use to relate to that customer +

show them the journey of how you transform them

The Hero wants to:

- Plan an event

- Learn how to write a book

- Go on a vacation

- Look their best

You'll **SHOW** them:

- What it's like to experience your event-from the hero's perspective - not the business!

- Your process of writing a book - what was that like for you? What will they experience? What should they avoid? How will they feel + how to avoid writer's block, etc...

- What each location can make them feel by showing them people who've gone there...their experiences, their recommendations + STORIES.

First, think what does that mean to the customer?

How do they want to look their best? Then, why you are that solution. SHOW LIFESTYLE!

When you tell the story, the story is about the HERO.

Everything that you discover then becomes your sales copy!

Now, Let's funnel that customer into a sale!

Relate to them through the branded visuals - that will be the entry point.

Goal: Get new customers/ leads into your business with each post!

Talk to them and build that relationship so that they legit can't live without you! (*Know factor*)

Obviously, they can.

But they don't want to!

These become the elements of your one page funnel.

This is how you will sell on Instagram, without burnout, without tons of money, and without posting to crickets.

Learn exactly how to create product offers from what you've learned. Combine:

- USP

- Brand Identity

- Value Content

- Trust Factor

And create a SIMPLE one page funnel. That is, a single page that combines all of these elements together as the product offer.

- No Website

- No Lead Pages

- No Shopify

- No GoDaddy

Notes + Thoughts

Instagram for Business:

v. *Product Offers*

V. Product Offers

Presenting the offers breakdown into stages:

Imagery (Branded presence)

Your branded presence is the entry point for your sales funnel.

You're going to need a consistent visual feed that draws your customer's attention. This is only for those who want to follow my system of drawing your ideal customer to you. That is, getting hundreds of follows with each post instead of chasing the customers.

You're putting the work to bring those audiences in; make sure that when they arrive, they see a feed that they want to follow + build a relationship with.

Just think; when you see certain feeds on Instagram, they pull you in. You're impressed by the visual appearance. It's no different for your dream customer.

Create a consistent color palette that you'll use to identify your brand look + design.

Avoid using graphics with tons of sales copy over them.

If you're going to sell, do it in the caption with your long form posts.

I use a posting strategy with each day's content:

2 posts are intended to go viral, and just draw in tons of my target audience.

So that would be content that's evoking an emotion: funny, serious, sassy…something that I know my audience will love, and they will begin to tag their friends, helping me reach hundreds, sometimes thousands of new followers on a single post.

The third post is for relating + relationship building with that audience, starting to zone in on my dream customer.

The final post is intended to sell.

Again, I will choose a photo that I know will convert well based on the data from previous posts. Then I make the caption long form value, usually with an invite into one of my courses or trainings.

I will also sometimes make other offers in those posts as well; ebooks, sales, etc.

Use a planning app to help you schedule your content. Even if you decide not to keep the schedule, you can plan out the feed design. Go the extra mile and you will attract customers who appreciate that extra, added effort.

Planoly is one of my favorites for achieving this. Give it a try!

Upsell funnels are an excellent way to add on to product offers. In fact, you can move from a single sale on each purchase to multiple purchases each time. Using a system like Samcart can help you do this.

Each product gets a matching product that adds value to the customer, and to your bottom line. Imagine each customer going from one product sale, to 3 for every single customer.

What would that feel like?

If you sell an ebook, you can see a hardcopy then a membership. Or sell a clutch, wrap, and set of earrings. The key is to multiply the sale with items that make sense to the consumer in an "upsell funnel", all automated for every visitor.

Kind of awesome, right?

You can check out a list of some of my favorite business startup resources on ThePoshGirlsClub website under Free Startup Kit. Most have free trials or are simply free to use.

Notes + Thoughts

Instagram for Business:

Lead Generation

BONUS: Lead Generation:

When I see my community members working on
bringing in new customers, I always wonder why their
voice changes in the written sales copy. And I think,
it's because we as marketing experts call it *"written
sales copy"*.

It sounds so formal and serious. And so, you tend to
switch to what I refer to as *"The Harvard Voice"*, and
the tone becomes so serious + formal.

You lose the part of you that your audience has come for. You become more focused on saying the right things, perfectly written or stated, and lose sight of the part that makes you the person they initially followed.

When you're putting together all of the materials that become lead generating sales copy, don't forget to remain *you*.

It's you that the audience wants to hear from. It's you that they want to hang out with and receive emails from.

And when they do open those emails up, they want them to sound just like you.

The person **they know, like, and trust**.

So, when you're composing that sales copy, think about these factors:

Your emails should sound more like you as the person driving the brand voice.

That's why creating your brand voice + identity matter up front in the brand development stages.

The emails should match that tone.

And it should be a consistent voice that the audience recognizes.

If you're posting funny content, that's what your emails should also reflect. Intense and broody?

Dealing with subject matter that's more serious and intended to tug at the heartstrings?

Guess what?

Your emails = more of that!

When you're serious and intense on your posts, then become silly and lighthearted in your emails, the customer wonders who this person is and how they ended up on that email list.

So, find your voice.

Keep it consistent.

As you write your posts, think about your dream customer. The posts that you add to your feed should always be consistent. If you're a business focused around health + nutrition, under no circumstances should any of your posts be *about "Netflixing and chilling in a pizza binge"*.

Under any circumstance!

That is, unless you're speaking against it or why that's bad for your health. It's just inconsistent, and your audience will feel that, too.

It doesn't matter at all how much you love the post. It sends the exact opposite message of your brand story + purpose.

Honestly, if you like it that much, post it on your personal feed.

Keep the voice of your brand consistent. This will build trust within your community and help set you up as the thought leader, or the ideal influencer in your space.

I watch newbies in the community, and even pages that I come across, and see the inconsistencies all the time.

I'll review the page and see that these types of pages are not intended for monetizing.

They're purely entertaining.

And while that may be great for the sake of just having an entertaining Instagram page...that's not *your* ultimate goal, right?

Take the time to identify the voice of your business and you'll spend less time trying to get to the right customer.

They'll find you.

They'll know you.

They will follow and then convert into sales.

Notes + Thoughts

Instagram for Business:

Free Resources + Lead Magnets

Free Resources + Lead Magnets

There is a system to giving out your freebies to the audience.

The resource should lead up to, or accompany your sell.

You're not giving away all of what you know or sell. You're

simply giving the potential customer a glimpse into the

experience of you/ your product.

Example:

You're a tee shirt company. You have different slogans + catchy quotes on them. The key is to show your visitor the style of the person who may want to wear that item.

An emerging trend guide or look book will give that visitor some value on how to style the item you want them to purchase.

Show them how it can be worn, with accessories, shoes, pants or skirts, etc. Give the user the full idea of how they can expect to use your item.

But show that with the individual out with friends, working out, etc. Whatever they'll do with your product on; lifestyle.

The other alternative could be a hair extensions brand. The draw, or value can be in a care tutorial. How would the individual take care of your hair extensions or even wigs, clip-ins, etc., for extended use. Show the person how they can save by preserving their product longer.

Many will be nervous about the buyer being able to use the product longer, which means longer for the next sale. But the opposite is what generally happens when done correctly; the person buys more.

Then they tell their friends, family, and anyone who asks about your business, because they know you are all about quality over quantity.

They'll invest more into you, because you're helping them to use your product better.

The lead magnet should inform, not solve.

In the information industry, coaching or authors, the lead magnet breaks down similarly.

Address the issues and concerns of the individual you're creating the solution for. This helps the person to see themselves in your business.

You will talk about their struggle and how you know they must be feeling based on that struggle that they are experiencing.

You will help them to develop an emotional connection to you through the free resource because they will start to see that you understand exactly where they are. But beyond that,

they will know that you understand where they would like to

go.

Or who they want to become.

 The free resource continues to break down your experience

with that exact thing. Or, the hero of your story, and how

they relate.

Then you tell them, or better yet, show them how you are the

solution to that problem they are experiencing.

So you don't give away your sell. You're not giving all the

answers to *how* you do whatever it is that might be revealed

in that coaching, or in that book or course. You simply give

an example about the fact that you helped the hero through

that *exact* thing. And how the hero is now thriving because of you.

So that is how you can give value to your audience and do live streams, Instagram stories, free discovery sessions and blog posts.

You focus on relating to the customer and letting them know that yes, I understand what you are experiencing.

Yes, I feel your pain and frustration with the lack of or need for what I have to help you with.

Because I've dealt with this person, or I was this person. And through this formula that I have for you or through this resource or book or through my coaching, I can help deliver you because I get it.

For any industry whether it is clothing, accessories, shoes, books or even services, this is the formula for a lead magnet.

Notes + Thoughts

Instagram for Business:

VI. *Relationship Building*

Relationship Building; Email Sequences

The email sequences are the balancing act in building customer relationships. Mail is not dead, and as far forward as I can see, it's never going away.

I've been writing emails so long, I feel like there can be books for a lifetime of monetizing, just in selling written copy. Only problem; I wasn't always great at it.

There's been an evolution in how I write them - and complete intention on the order and strategy of putting them together. People often ask *"how many emails are too many"*?

My question becomes, *"well, how much money do you want to make?"*

The answer to that isn't about the amount of emails you send. Rather, in the quality of emails you send. The goal with your email writing is to build the connection.

Ideally, you'll need to focus on creating specific, intentional messages that follow a purposeful strategy.

One of my methods for creating effective emails is to write out the plan for the sequence. Literally identify the ultimate goal of the email funnel.

First, always think about the individual product offer. What is the story you're connecting to that offer? You know, the journey of your hero.

How are you moving the customer along in the journey? What do they want to achieve? How do you help them to do this?

Write all of the journey out and then create bullet points for each email. Then, you can begin writing the copy for each one.

Your journey becomes so much clearer. And you can deliver value in them while making offers for your products in each one.

The customer sees the journey of the hero. And in various parts of the funnel, they can decide when they are ready to opt in - and if you do this right, it's sooner than later that your conversions begin.

From there, you can move the customer further into your other product offerings.

The ultimate goal is to build that customer relationship, while cultivating new ones (*on auto*).

How many emails are too many?

That's an ongoing question I hear. Here's my forever answer:

Forget the size of the list, *follow the conversions*!

There are people with millions of names on their email list. But a very small percentage of those people are converting.

Very often, these are even competitors, on-lookers, and what I refer to as "fans" (*people who swear they don't like you, but really want to see what you're doing*), depending on the type of business you have; especially those successful businesses.

I tend to go in quarterly and move most of my list, the non-conversions, to a list outside of my main one.

I want to be certain that all of the people, or most, are those truly interested in the content and wanting to purchase.

Those who want to buy are always active in my stories and on my website, Instagram feed, etc.

They check in with me consistently daily or weekly.
I'm not losing customers by doing this. Instead, I'm keeping fresh lists and leads engaged through classes, offers, my private communities, etc.

You will decide how often to purge your audience. And while you may not want to get rid of everyone, you can focus on the main, most engaged audiences. I'm not saying to completely get rid of them. After all, they may convert over time.

I'm simply saying, to make sure that you're building a list of those (*and maintaining*) who are converting in your company.

Don't focus on how many emails you send.

The key is defining a full plan for those who opt in. Then make the emails quality messages that naturally, they want to continue receiving.

And remember; if people leave the list, most likely, they weren't going to buy anyway.

And they just may not be ready to purchase yet, in preparation mode.

There are those who'll come for the free information, resource, or product and that's okay. Operate from the concept of what I refer to as, ***the open hand***.

Notes + Thoughts

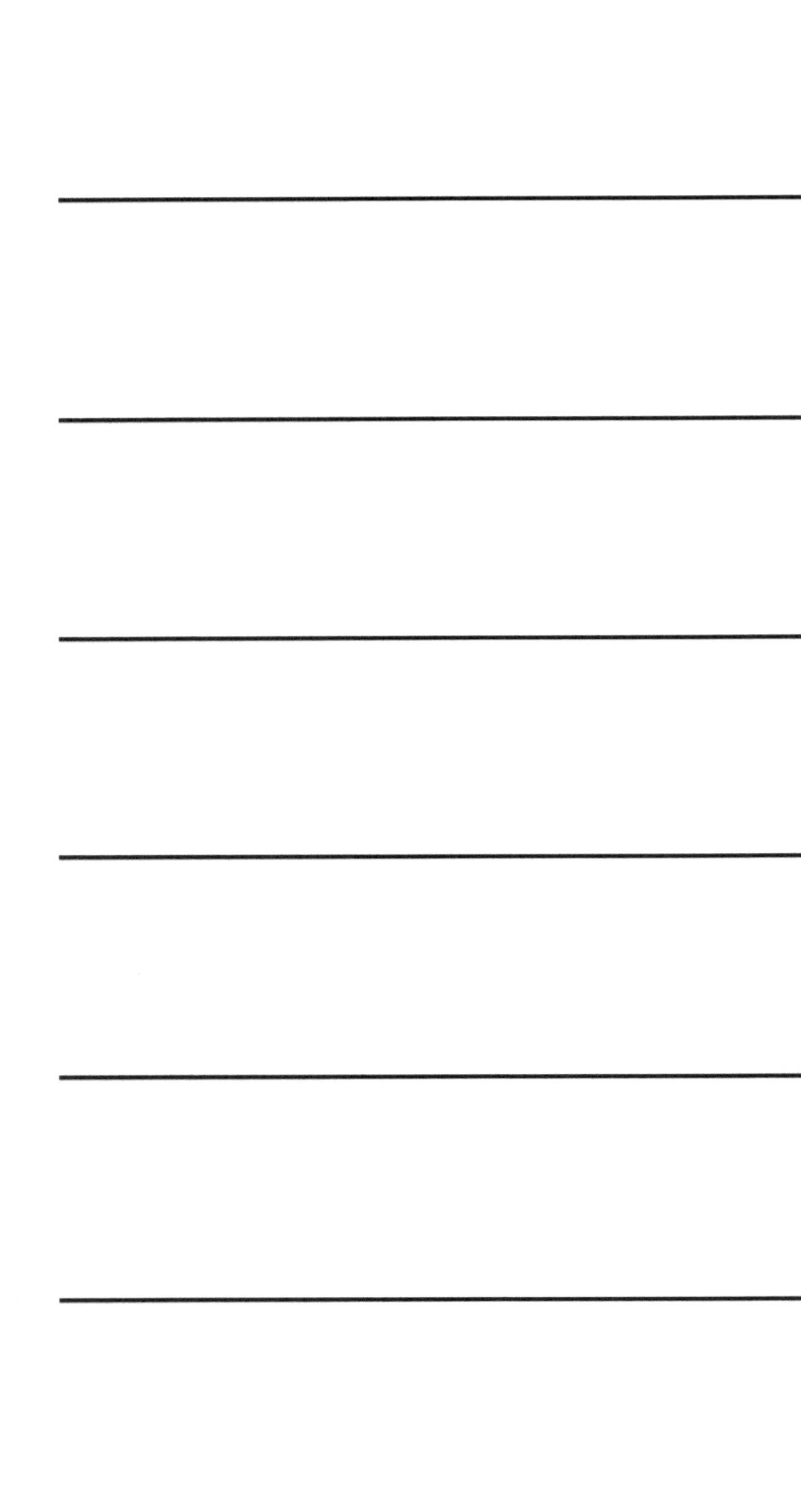

Instagram for Business:

VII. Launch

VII. **Your Launch**

Your launch is the next step. It's always important to collect leads first. That means, deliver value to the consumer that is directly related to your offer. Tons of it.

I never take the word of someone who is afraid to give value. Why? Because there is so much to know and share about what I know, I always have more value to give; Always.

I know that I can talk about that product (service) ongoing, indefinitely, without fail.

I know that I can deliver value to a thousand people on how to do something for free. I also know that half of them will need my help with the execution.

So if 500 of them took my advice and tips to do something, and they go on and do it on their own - great!

There are 500 who will need me to help them do *the thing*. And that original 500 who opted to go it alone may need me in the next stage.

Share value and help people use your product. Don't worry about the competitors or lurkers who joined your list to simply "see".

Because they aren't you. They can get a part of what you

have to share.

And you'll still be out there, winning regardless of what they

come to replicate from your business.

Instagram for Business:

The Recap

I've identified some of the most important, key elements of how you will use Instagram to begin building your audience and growing your business.

This series of steps is exactly what major influencers like the Kardashian brand and family, Huda Beauty, and Fashion Nova, and me here @ThePoshGirlsClub have used to create massive success.

First you draw interest in the product you want to offer. That can be an individual, digital, or a tangible item.

Next, deliver value in a series of communications and relationship building with your audience.

Then you present them with offers that they are open to receive because they have found a connection with you through your branding, your content, and you showing up dearly and being completely consistent with whatever that brand of voice is.

Now, you can deliver them upsell offers and make ongoing sales through that trust that you've built with that audience.

And that will lead to Influence.

Perhaps live events, brand partnerships, and the ability to grow at whatever scale you have set in your mind.

Is it always my goal to give you value, because I want to see you win. I want to see your brands thrive and you create the life that you always imagined you could and would live.

Keep hustling, girls.

XO, Tori

Join our Business Community:

https://www.facebook.com/groups/poshgirlsclub/

www.ingramcontent.com/pod-product-compliance
Lightning Source LLC
Chambersburg PA
CBHW022008170526
45157CB00003B/1190